The Journey

Jessica Blowers

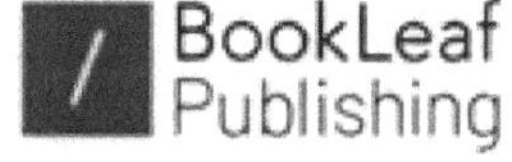
BookLeaf Publishing

The Journey © 2022 Jessica Blowers

All rights reserved.

No part of this publication may be reproduced, stored in a retrieval system, or transmitted, in any form or by any means, electronic, mechanical, photocopying, recording or otherwise, without the prior written permission of the presenters.

Jessica Blowers asserts the moral right to be identified as author of this work.

Presentation by *BookLeaf Publishing*

Web: www.bookleafpub.com

E-mail: info@bookleafpub.com

ISBN: 9789357210546

First edition 2022

DEDICATION

I would like to dedicate this book to my children: Madison, Saturn, and Taylor. The work is important because you all are important to me. I love you. Thank you for everything you have done and continue to do for me.

ACKNOWLEDGEMENT

I would like to thank my ACA family for your support and encouragement. Without you, I would not have rediscovered the voice of my inner child.
I would like to acknowledge my parents for giving me life, but I thank Higher Power for giving me strength.
Thank you to my friends for believing in me. I appreciate you all more than you know.

PREFACE

This poetic journey started a few years ago. Though it begins with a breakup and reunion, this is only the catalyst that led me to understanding how my life had become unmanageable. Through the ACA program, I have found a way to dig myself out of the hole that I found myself in. It felt as though I had been in a place between sleep and waking, living my life but mostly on autopilot. Once I woke to my plight, I had to struggle (have to struggle) daily to keep recovery from the past. It is my hope to bring a light to your darkness. The sun is bright in my life - sometimes a blessing and sometimes a curse. But, one thing is for sure, I cannot return to sleeping.

Thank you for taking the time to read these poems.

What I Thought was the Beginning of the End

Currently, unerringly inflamed
By the feelings yet unidentified.
Anyone would be pained
To consider all that is denied
In the relationship contained
between the desires aligned
In the love un-attained.

His name I had denied
Before I had ascertained
The words he'd said were lies.
His love had not abstained
And though my pillow felt my cries
My heart he had not disdained.
My love had been allied.

A Bottom

Years passed.
Time moved on.
My love would last,
But I had to be gone.

I yearned to understand
How it all began.
I longed to command
God to keep my man

But a journey was required
To understand myself.
It has lit a fire
To take me off the shelf.

I examine each broken piece
And the puzzle I try to assemble.
I want to have the same lease
On life that once I remembered.

Battle

And so the pieces lay.
They do not care
How I find the way.

I must be diligent as I prepare.
I cannot take a single day
To linger - I have to beware.

Around every corner seems to lurk
The vortex that wants to draw me in.
Each day, I strive to do the ACA work.

There are moments of light
That give me some hope,
But then comes the night.

Stay Awake

The vortex is awake.
It is a thing with life.
This thing makes me shake.
It makes me long for night.

Before I found the work
I felt like one asleep.
There were moments of hurt
But everything was not bleak.

Though it is the same now,
I still sometimes long to return
To when I would allow
Myself to be less concerned.

I feel the pull of sleep.
I feel the draw to give up.
It is so hard for me to keep
Myself out of the rut.

I must find a safe place
With peacefulness and joy.
I look for this space
For my inner child to employ.

Conversations

A day to try something new
Because the inner critic's voice
In my head so loud makes me blue.
I quietly asked amid all the noise,
"What can I possibly do for you?"

The voice settled down for a moment.
There was silence inside for once.
Then a word entered my conscience.
It said, "safety." I felt like a dunce.

Sardonically, I nodded and smiled.
The critic's anger is understandable.
With its emotional range of a child,
Our communication is incompatible.

The day started to feel lighter.
My anxiety symptoms were less.
I started to feel like a fighter.
I will continue to do my best.

The Matrix

The Matrix isn't just a popular film.
Similar to the vortex, in many ways
It seeks and pulls to draw me further in.
But it is easier to resist most days.

Technology is not how I see the matrix.
It is a much more subtle and hidden thing.
It tells me to get back to the basics -
Financial security and maybe a wedding ring.

There were so many things in my life
That I simply was not taught to do.
These things that other children might
Start earlier on and then continue.

A college education was not mentioned
Until I was quite late in the game.
Little did I know that a student's intention
Should be set up years before - lame.

So I squandered and frittered money away.
These were loans - not free cash to use.
I figured I would worry about it someday.
But that large bill has now come due.

Regardless of whether or not I pay
The exorbitant minimum payments
They have set for some other day,
Their existence is a derailment.

I cannot get a home loan.
I cannot rent an apartment.
I continue ruminating on
My many, many resentments.

Not It

A poet is not something I ever
Would have willingly called myself.
The ability to rhyme, however,
Seems to flow like nothing else.

My kids have taken to calling me
The name of a famous poet.
His rhymes always guarantee
Recognition in a mere moment.

I wish I had his talent and range.
I wish I had any abilities at all.
I often feel like one deranged.
I am quite near the great fall.

Pipe Dreams

My friend calls me a dreamer.
Each day holds one that's new.
I think of myself as a schemer.
My mind needs something to do.

The first thought was a tent.
I could just buy some land.
Done with barely a cent,
It's the first to come to hand.

The next thought was a bus.
I thought kids liked van life.
However, that was a bust.
It only brought me strife.

My next thought was to build
A house with scrap materials.
The space would be filled
Faster than a bowl of cereal.

These dreams are wasted time.
I don't have the energy or funds
To complete these tasks and I'm
Running low on rhyming puns.

Suessical

The point I'm trying to make
By referencing Suess and dreams
Is that my life makes me ache.
And I'm running out of schemes.

The fact is that I would live
In any situation that I could
As long as I am able to have
My kids just as I should.

We could live in any house
As long as it isn't haunted.
We could live with a mouse
If that's what they wanted.

I would take them anywhere
It really doesn't matter to me.
We could go here or there
So long as I can say "we."

Promises

"I promise, it will get better,"
I hear everyone keep saying.
But could they put it in a letter?
'Cause my faith keeps straying.

It's hard to see a clear picture
When fires keep popping up.
I'm tired of hearing the lecture
About the damn half empty cup.

Optimism won't give me sanity.
Please don't say I'll get stronger.
I just want to scream profanities.
Can I really hold on much longer?

Each day, however, holds some light.
They're not a Neverending dull gray.
The light makes me think that I might
Simply survive and make it another day.

Acting Out

Today I see the raindrops fall.
The weather matches my mood.
My feelings are behind a wall.
They are masked with wanting food.

I think back upon my childhood
When I thought I ate out of boredom.
I hadn't considered that I could
Process my feelings or even sort 'em.

As I have started the ACA program
I am aware of the many ways we can
Ignore feelings that are so crammed
Inside our sad hearts. However, I am

Trying to see the ways that I act out,
Instead of ignoring them like I have.
Television, books, sex, food, or about
A million ways to pretend I'm not sad.

Friend or Foe?

Anxiety seems to be a constant friend.
A companion I'm not sure that I asked for.
It feels like it will be here til the end.
But my body surely can't take much more.

Sometimes it's there without a reason.
I can't put my finger on why I feel
So much like I have certainly done
Something to make me feel off keel.

I must remind myself over and over
What's done is done and all I can
Do is what I can do. Please lower
The heightened sense of this damn

Panic, please. I'm jealous of other people.
They never seem to worry about all the
Many things I can't let go. It's not illegal
To not worry, simply exist, and just be me.

I Need You

Higher Power, to me, is something that's elusive.
Though I strive and continue to seek it daily,
I tend to wonder if membership is exclusive.
I know I need to access it to stop this ailing.

The moments when its power is clearest to me
Are the moments when I feel a deep swirling in
my chest. I think it's where my soul would be.
Gives me solace to feel, I just never know when

I will enter that soothing space and find peace.
Mindfulness and meditation are supposed to
Help one reach that place inside and to cease
The chattering voice in the mind. In order to do

The unthinkable - and shut that voice right up,
I would do a great deal. But it seems to be a
Vicious cycle. Meditation will fill one's cup
But I need patience in order to sit and stay.

Letting Go?

A common thing that I have heard
Throughout my life has been to let
Go and let God. But that "g" word
Is loaded. It hasn't been a safe bet.

The past hasn't shown me there's
Any rhyme or reason to how my
Life will or will not go. Where's
My happy ending? The stories lie.

It's so hard to just let go. I feel
Like I wasn't holding on tightly
To any one plan or goal. But real
Trauma has been almost nightly.

Why is it that some can have the
Life that others only dream of?
Can someone just answer me?
I want to build a life that I love.

A Prayer

"What's wrong?" she quietly asked me.
"Just in my head," was my only reply.
"Well, stop." I really wish I could be
Free from the thoughts that plague my
Mind. My thoughts won't let me see
A possibility of letting go. I only cry.

My codependency has hold of everything.
The inner critic wants us to find safety.
It's running the show. I can't even bring
The madness to a slow down. Completely
Absorbed in the thoughts - they string
Me along and keep me occupied with me.

It makes me feel selfish. There are so
Many people in situations like mine.
I see the homeless people - I have no
Money or help to offer - not a dime.
The yawning hole in me only grows.
It's consuming. I just need more time.

"But it's been a month," he says to me.
"Yes, just a month," apparently is not
An appropriate response for him. He
Only wants what's best for me. A lot

Of people do. But some can really see
That I am trying. "Lazy?" I'm just not.

I fight through the pain and fatigue to keep
Going. Strangely, I still feel lucky today.
The mountain that I had to climb was steep -
Metaphorically, anyway. I want to stay
In my body - please don't go back to sleep.
Please just let the madness stay at bay

Heaviness

"Weeping with rage," is something I never
thought
That I would do. My intense feelings will not
Allow me to get through a day without sobs.
It just feels like the universe decided to lob
Rotten vegetables at me - like an old theater
Audience or political protest. It may be neater.

I fall to my knees in agony when I consider
The hole I've dug for myself. Life's littered
With the trash of my poor decisions. Really,
I'm exhausted and can't stand the many silly
Problems that plague me. I must take my own
Advice. It's something that I've always known.

I told my child just last night through tears,
"With life there's possibility." Some years
Are harder to stomach than others though.
Another one that pops up, "be still and know
That I am God." That quote's the hardest one
For me to follow now. My heart weighs a ton.

Hopeful

Every day is a new opportunity to find hope.
Most days I wake in a state of contentment,
But soon thoughts start to race. Can't cope.
If I can find one thing, though, they relent.

There will be some form of a silver lining
To the rain clouds that have become my life.
I will seek that silver and keep reminding
Myself that hope will come from the strife.

I cannot know the how, when, or where,
But I can tell the universe all my troubles.
It's up to it when it will decide to share
The brilliance shining up from the puddle.

I believe in a power greater than myself.
It holds me close when I can't hold on.
It's the ace in the hand that life has dealt.
Though it's hard to see, of me it is fond.

This power will bring me some clarity
And help me to navigate the choppy
Waters that I found myself in. Rarely
Will it let me go on without stopping

To appreciate the little things that I can see
And hear and smell throughout my day.
I seek the power, though. It doesn't seek me.
If I don't seek it daily, it will just stay away.

Collaboration with Saturn

"Do you remember why you're here my child?"
the Universe asks me.
Though I was wary of answering the call I
couldn't let it be.
I so desperately wanted to bask in the eternal
light,
finally feeling a sense of home during my lonely
nights.
I feel a severe in my communication with the
goddess.

Most days I simply ache to give up the endless
fight.
Instead of answering that, of course, the
Universe is right
I admit that I'm tired. "How much longer?" I ask.
"Not yet, love, you haven't yet completed the
task.
There are things you can learn about the
goddess."

I know this answer by heart, but I'm so tired of
trying.
It's so hard, some days it just feels like I'm just
dying.

"I miss you and want to be with you," I whisper.
The Universe says, "The goddess wants you
with her,
And you must accept the answer of the
goddess."

I feel so much lighter in knowing I have a
purpose.
It's just so hard to see it when all I have is the
surface.
I asked for reassurance from the universal
oneness.
"You promise?" I feel the Universe smiling. "Of
course.
I would never lie to you, especially about the
goddess. "

I must express my thanks and try to never forget
The beautiful promises from this conversation
and yet
I know there will be times when I cannot recall
The peace I feel when I can communicate with it
all.
I am thankful that I know I am needed by the
goddess.

If It's Meant to Be

Today I'm struck by the birds that Jesus spoke
about
They do not sow or reap or stow away in barns
The book of Matthew tells the many people
devout.
Though not a particular person to follow the
yarns
Spun by those biblical writers, I must agree with
The sentiment expressed. They are almost my
kith.

I have grown up listening to the many teachings
Established therein. Though I may not exactly
follow
The creed handed down, I must agree in
reaching
Out to a power greater than myself and just
allow
The peace that passes all understanding to wash
Away my fears and doubts. I must hoard and
stash

The possibilities in my heart to not lose that
hope.

Goddess, Universe, oneness - please grant me the
Ability to discern the right path for me and to cope
With whatever answer you give. What will be
Will be.

www.ingramcontent.com/pod-product-compliance
Lightning Source LLC
Chambersburg PA
CBHW070727160726
48003CB00006BA/2404